Compiled by Julia Skinner
With particular reference to the work of Henry Hall

THE FRANCIS FRITH COLLECTION

www.francisfrith.com

First published in the United Kingdom in 2006 by The Francis Frith Collection®

This edition published in 2014
ISBN 978-1-84589-759-8

British Library Cataloguing in Publication Data

Did You Know? Belfast - A Miscellany
Compiled by Julia Skinner
With particular reference to the work of Henry Hall.

The Francis Frith Collection
6 Oakley Business Park,
Wylye Road, Dinton,
Wiltshire SP3 5EU
Tel: +44 (0) 1722 716 376
Email: info@francisfrith.co.uk

www.francisfrith.com

Printed and bound in England

Front Cover: **BELFAST, BOTANIC GARDENS CONSERVATORY 1936** 87687p

The colour-tinting is for illustrative purposes only, and is not intended to be historically accurate

AS WITH ANY HISTORICAL DATABASE, THE FRANCIS FRITH ARCHIVE IS CONSTANTLY BEING CORRECTED AND IMPROVED, AND THE PUBLISHERS WOULD WELCOME INFORMATION ON OMISSIONS OR INACCURACIES

CONTENTS

INTRODUCTION

The second largest city in Ireland, just over 100 miles north of Dublin, Belfast is the capital of Northern Ireland, the ancient province of Ulster. It was no ancient town; the earliest settlement in the area began to develop after Sir Arthur Chichester was given the small castle by the river and the surrounding lands in 1603. The growth of marketing and trading in the area, particularly of textiles, helped a port to develop, but Belfast is really a city born of the industrial revolution, with extensive docks, ship-building and heavy industry.

The 1st Marquess of Donegall was responsible for laying the elegant architectural and prosperous financial foundations of 18th-century Belfast. The centre is based around Donegall Square, including the magnificent City Hall and the Linen Hall library. Other notable buildings include both Protestant and Catholic churches, and the Victorian Queen's University. South of the city are the Botanic Gardens.

In the 1770s cotton, then a protected Irish industry, yielded to manufacture by machinery; it was in Belfast that there was the business acumen and the capital to build the first Irish cotton mill. More mills followed, and then linen manufacture became mechanised, with Belfast supplying a world-wide market. By 1897 the local mills employed something like 50,000 workers, giving the city its name of 'Linenapolis'.

Apart from the linen industry, the other major source of employment in 19th-century Belfast was the shipbuilding industry: the largest yard employed nearly 9,000 men who delivered eleven sizeable ships during 1897. Outside the yards there were also several engineering works supplying the world.

After bearing the brunt of the Troubles of the 20th century, the city and the riverfront of Belfast are now being transformed into a vibrant, busy modern environment. Much of the city centre is pedestrianised, and is often lively and colourful with street musicians. The £320m retail centre of Victoria Square is one of Europe's largest regeneration projects. Many of Belfast's exuberant Victorian and Edwardian buildings have survived, some of which feature elaborate sculptures over doors and windows of gods and poets, scientists, kings and queens, peering down from the high ledges of banks and old linen warehouses.

The story of Belfast is full of fascinating characters and events, of which this book can only provide a brief glimpse.

THE BOTANIC GARDENS 1897 40212

BELFAST WORDS AND PHRASES

(With thanks to Mr Calvert Jones for his assistance with these items)

'Geg' - Joke.

'Gutties' - Plimsoles.

'Duncher' - Cloth Cap.

'Skitter' - A cheeky person.

'Glype' - A person always doing things wrong.

'Skelp' - Smack.

'I hit him a quare skelp on the gub' - I hit him quite a slap on the face.

'Yer man's a quare geg' - He's very funny.

'He thinks he's the fella in the big picture' - Describing someone who is arrogant.

'He's as broad between the shoulders as herrin' between the eyes' - Describing somebody of slim build.

'What fut does he kick with?' - What religion is he?

'He was cut to the bone' - He was very embarrassed.

'He's that mean he would skin a louse for its coat' - An ungenerous person.

HAUNTED BELFAST

A building located in a former Irish Linen mill in Belfast's Linen Conservation area which now houses a printing firm is believed to be haunted by the ghost of a 16-year-old girl, who has been identified as Helena Blunden. Records show that she died after a tragic accident in the building on 14 April 1912, apparently breaking her neck after tripping on a floor brush left at the top of a flight of stairs. Helena died on the very day that the 'Titanic' sank; ironically, a few months earlier she and other employees in the mill had been making tablecloths for the first-class dining room on the liner. In 1998 a live web-cam was installed in the building, and many viewers reported seeing Helena's apparition. Ghostly footsteps have also been heard in the building.

The spectre of a lady has been reported in Vicarage Street; she walks down the street carrying a cup in one hand and a cigarette in the other, so she presumably dates from the 20th century!

A well near Carrickfergus Castle is traditionally haunted by the ghost of an old soldier known as Buttercup who was executed after a case of mistaken identity; his name comes from the large button worn on his head dress.

One of Belfast's most famous stories is that of James Haddock. When he died in 1657, James left part of his land to his wife Arminell, and the rest to go to his son when he reached the age of 21. The executor of the will was Daniel Davis, who married Arminell several years later. Daniel and Arminell had a son of their own, and Daniel altered the will in his favour instead of James's son. A few years later, a great friend of James Haddock, one Francis Tavener, was riding over Drum Bridge on the outskirts of south Belfast when his horse reared up, frightened by a ghost which Francis recognised as James. The apparition warned Francis to take Daniel Davis to court over the matter of the will, and appeared several times to Francis until, at last, he took Daniel Davis to court in Carrickfergus. The court usher called for James Haddock to appear several times to no avail, until at last a shrouded hand rose from the witness box, and a voice boomed out 'Is this enough?' The case was proved, and Daniel was found guilty. James Haddock's grave is in Drumbeg parish churchyard, where his gravestone refuses to remain upright.

BELFAST MISCELLANY

There were already several schools in the town when the Minister of the First Presbyterian Church in Belfast advertised the arrival of a new academy. It could take boarders, and must have been intended for the middle classes. The first school building was constructed not too far from the church in what was to become Academy Street. Discipline was strict, which caused a revolt when some boys took food from the kitchen and barricaded themselves in, armed with pistols. Armed men were brought to force a way in. Situated at the corner with Donegall Street and very near the parish church, the first Academy was in a pleasant enough part of town. It was not to stay that way, and no provision had been made for privacy or expansion. During the course of the 19th century the street filled with the homes of skilled workers, along with a variety of yards and a wash-house. The numbers of pupils fell dramatically. All this was put right in 1878, when the move was made to the fine building seen in photograph 87676, opposite, about one and a half miles out of town, and set in the new suburbs along the Cliftonville Road.

The name Belfast originates from the Irish 'Béal Feirste', or 'the mouth of the Farset', the river on which the city was built. The River Farset now languishes under the High Street in obscurity, superseded by the River Lagan in importance.

ROYAL ACADEMY 1936 87676

HIGH STREET 1897 40176

The broad thoroughfare of High Street, seen in photograph 40176 (above), reflects not only the market town but also its links with the sea. Below the cobbles still runs the River Farset, which once had quays allowing ships to come off the Lagan. The far, tall building in the photograph marks Bridge Street, the spot where the first bridge upstream was located.

The broad, straight streets of Belfast tell of land reclaimed from former rivers and docks as part of the city's development. Its quays were once the heart of Belfast the port, and there is no doubt that the remains of Chichester Quay and Hanover Quay would be found below the cobblestones of Queen's Square. Some of the Square's very old houses survived until recently, but air raids in 1941 destroyed the fine Georgian buildings opposite the Custom House.

During the 19th century the well-laid-out streets to the south of Belfast beyond Donegall Square were matched by those built on the reclaimed land near York Street. In between, there remained a triangle of small slum streets beginning at Castle Place. In 1878 the Town Council obtained powers to clear the area; they began by extending the town centre with a fine new street connecting Castle Place with York Street. There was already the beginnings of a route in one very old narrow street, but all signs of Hercules Street were to disappear, along with its 40 fleshers and their killing yard. Four thousand people were to lose their homes, but it was said that they would have no difficulty in finding somewhere else to go. The thoroughfare was to be 80ft wide, and lined with tall buildings built to a uniform height, fronted with shops to create a first-rate retailing zone. The result was Royal Avenue. On the left of photograph 40186, below, is the Provincial Bank, behind its railings and shrubs: this was listed among the five best bank buildings in Belfast. Next to it is the imposing building of the Ulster Reform Club.

ROYAL AVENUE 1897 40186

THE 'DYNAMIC' 1897 40230

The ship seen in this photograph was one of a fleet of six owned by the Belfast Steamship Company. She was one of its express boats, which provided a nightly service from Liverpool to Donegall Quay; cargo went from York Dock. Behind can be seen the crammed yard of Harland and Wolff, where the 'Dynamic' had been built fourteen years earlier. In 1897 eleven new ships were delivered from this yard, including the 'Pennsylvania' for the Hamburg Amerika Line - according to the Belfast Newsletter, the largest in the world.

THE GLASGOW BOAT 1897 40233

The Royal Mail Steamer 'Adder' seen in photograph 40233, above, made the link with Glasgow by sailing to Ardrossan. This avoided the long journey along the Clyde Estuary - the route was completed by rail. For this daylight crossing, the train will have left Glasgow Central at 9.07am with passengers arriving at Princes Quay at 4pm. The vessel was not very old; perhaps conditions at Ardrossan dictated the use of paddle propulsion at a time when screw had become the norm.

The Albert Clock Tower was built on swampy ground, and the foundations were not adequate. A tilt developed and the tower is now 4½ft off base. It is known as the Leaning Tower of Belfast!

The White Linen Hall, where linen was bought and sold, was built in 1783; the City Hall stands on the site today.

The statue in Hillsborough's Main Street (see photograph H142006, below) is of the 4th Marquess of Downshire, the eleventh descendant of the Hills of Hillsborough; he inherited large estates throughout Ireland, as well as in England. His term as Marquess also coincided with the great famine of the mid 19th century. The Marquess did not leave Ireland, stating 'I will stand by the people and attend to their wants even should I be obliged to mortgage my last acre'.

HILLSBOROUGH, MAIN STREET c1890 H142006

In its early years Belfast was firmly under the control of Sir Arthur Chichester. When he became Lord Deputy of Ireland, Belfast was made one of the 40 new Irish boroughs, which were each able to send two members of parliament to Dublin. Both of Belfast's members were the choice of the Chichester family for several generations. By the end of the 17th century the head of this powerful family was given the title of Lord Donegall, and there are still street names everywhere which recall this event.

Queen Victoria was 42 when her consort, Prince Albert, died. She grieved her loss for the rest of her life and many towns and cities built monuments to the prince. For Belfast the monument had to be fitting and the subscription generous. The statue of Prince Albert is 40ft above the ground, and the clock tower was given a bell weighing nearly 2 tonnes. The clockwork is to the same design as that of London's Big Ben. The clock's central position at the foot of High Street meant diverting the underground River Farset. The clock mechanism of the Albert Clock was made by the local chronometer makers F M Moore, whose premises were in the High Street. The accuracy of the time shown on the 10ft dials was kept under observation by the firm with the aid of an electric signal box from Greenwich, using the under-sea Telegraphic Cabling System.

At one time Belfast not only had the largest flax-spinning mill in the world, but also boasted the world's largest ropeworks and the world's largest purpose-built tobacco factory.

QUEEN'S SQUARE 1897 40178

CORN MARKET 1897 40184

The street name Corn Market reminds us of Belfast the market town. Photograph 40184, above, shows the view from Arthur Square (a name recalling the Chichester family). Since the famine and the ending of the restrictive Corn Laws, grain was largely an import handled by a number of merchants. The curved building was brand new at the time this photograph was taken.

Belfast's Poor House of 1774 was built 'for the employment of idle beggars … and for the reception of old and diseased poor'. Children were later admitted and it was thanks to them being 'employed' with spinning wheels that Belfast's first cotton mill was born.

The Methodist College (photograph 40199, below) was built in response to an urgent need for a school for the sons of Methodist ministers, for the ministers were re-located every three years. A Limerick architect provided the design of the building, though his estimates of cost proved to be low - help from American Methodists in meeting construction costs was welcome. The college opened in 1868, taking 80 boarders and 120 day boys, not all Methodists. It soon became the largest school in Belfast. Some years later, additional accommodation was provided in the McArthur Hall; this was named after its benefactor, who was Lord Mayor of London and a Westminster MP.

THE METHODIST COLLEGE 1897 40199

HIGH STREET 1897 40175

The forest of poles seen above 16 High Street in this photograph marks the telephone exchange, staffed by operators waiting for incoming calls before pushing the plug to make the connection.

THE ISLE OF MAN STEAMER 1897 40232

Photograph 40232, above, shows the Royal Mail steamer plying to the Isle of Man: it had just left the quay at Belfast at 4pm. On summer Sundays there was more work to be done by the boat, with 'Holiday Tours' to Liverpool or Dublin calling at Douglas on the Isle of Man.

The Belfast Newsletter is the oldest weekly newspaper in the world still in publication. It was founded in 1737.

Belfast Castle is superbly situated a few miles to the north of the city, on Castle Hill overlooking Belfast Lough. It was built in 1870 by the 3rd Marquess of Donegall, and was given to the city in 1934.

The Belfast trams are in evidence in photograph 40187a, below. The gauge was 4ft 8in, rather than the Irish standard of 5ft 3in. The last tram ran in 1954, but trolleybuses continued until 1968.

CASTLE PLACE 1897 40187a

CASTLE PLACE 1897 40187

Horse-drawn trams were a long established feature of the city. The 114 cars and 1,000 horses were the property of the Belfast Street Tramway Company. By the time of photograph 40187 (above) the system was still being extended up the Cregagh and Anderstown Roads. All parts could be reached from this corner, and its popular name of Castle Junction had become fixed.

The Tropical Ravine in the Botanic Gardens was created in 1886 by Charles McKim, the curator of the gardens. It was said of McKim that he was so green-fingered that he could raise a prize bloom from a seed planted in an empty flower pot.

Donaghadee is a small town on the east coast of County Down, about seven miles east of Belfast. As one of the closest points to Scotland the harbour, designed by John Rennie, was once a thriving little port with a mail service to Portpatrick on the Wigtownshire coast. It lost that business to Larne in the mid 19th century, and is today a pleasant seaside and harbour town, with an old pub once visited by Peter the Great of Russia and the poet John Keats.

DONAGHADEE, BEACH 1897 40285

QUEENS COLLEGE 1897 40201

When the building seen in photograph 40201, above, was opened in 1849, Queens College was one of three set up by the government which were linked to the Royal University of Ireland, which operated as an examining body from Dublin. The other two colleges were at Cork and Galway. The object was to increase the supply of men with higher education, and it was hoped to attract entrants from all religions, with no theology being taught. Facilities were to be made available to all churches to instruct their own students. As it was, there was the 250-year-old Trinity College in Dublin under the control of the Established Church, and the Catholics had been provided with Maynooth College in 1795. In the recent past the northern Presbyterians had been refused government help to erect their own co-establishment to prepare men for the ministry, and were building their own nearby. They then provided Queens with its president and deputy president, as well as a number of lecturers. The Catholic Church would not support Queens at all. The photograph shows all that was built at the beginning; there is no evidence yet of local pride in the shape of buildings paid for by industry, including the Harland Engineering Laboratory. Eleven years after this view was taken, the independent Queens University of Belfast was created.

Two Belfast women, Betty Williams and Mairead Corrigan, were awarded the Nobel Peace Prize in 1976 for their work as cofounders of Community of Peace People, an organisation dedicated to promoting a peaceful resolution to the Troubles in Northern Ireland.

Photograph 87674, below, shows the beginning of the Lagan Canal; the boats are moored just above No 1 lock, the first of 27 needed to reach Lough Neagh. The smoking chimneys tell of the cramped homes of the river people - in their parlance they were at 'Molly Ward's Lock'. Up to this point the barges had navigated the wide, tidal river above the Belfast coal quays pulled by steam-engined tugs.

THE LAGAN CANAL, STRANMILLIS 1936 87674

Photograph 40221, below, shows the elevation to Donegall Quay, with the entrance for the masters of ocean-going ships, coming to report their arrival with goods which had to pay duty. This photograph also shows the Grand Central Hotel's courtesy coach waiting for visitors.

THE CUSTOM HOUSE 1897 40221

LARNE, THE VIEW FROM THE PROMENADE 1900 L142010

The linen manufacturing town of Larne (photograph L142010, above) which lies at the southern end of the magnificent Antrim Coast Road and close to the famous Glens of Antrim, is best known as the ferry terminal for the shortest crossing to the British mainland (Stranraer). The harbour is guarded by the 95ft-high Chaine memorial tower, which looks ancient but is a 19th-century reproduction of a round tower, to commemorate a local MP. The Curran, a promontory south of the town, was an important site for flint implement manufacture in Neolithic times.

Alexandra Park was the third park in Belfast. It opened in 1885, named after the Princess of Wales (later Queen Alexandra) who visited Belfast with the Prince of Wales (later Edward VII) in 1885.

The River Lagan flows within a few miles of the huge Lough Neagh, which is bordered by four Ulster counties. A lot of work was done to make the river able to take barges, with a link to the lough. Most of the traffic carried coal, which was loaded in the harbour beyond the bridge and taken to the linen mills along the river, but there was also a steady flow of sand downstream to this wharf. The barges made the first part of their journey upstream with the aid of steam tugs. In photograph 40225, below, we see a tug returning to the coal quays - its funnel would be lowered to miss the arches.

CANAL WHARF AND QUEEN'S BRIDGE 1897 40225

THE HARBOUR OFFICE 1897 40220

The Harbour Office (photograph 40220, above) was the office of the Harbour Commissioners, a body of senior ship owners, shippers and merchants. The Harbour Office was well furnished, in a style which was reminiscent of a London gentlemen's club, with marble busts and the walls hung with pictures. The Commissioners designed themselves a uniform for formal occasions: frock coats, white waistcoats and fancy buttons with gilt anchors. The Harbour Commissioners did away with the small docks to provide spaces on reclaimed land now occupied by Queen's, Albert and Corporation Squares. They established the basis of the present harbour; a major task was the cutting of the Victoria Channel to give a straight passage from Queen's Bridge to the Lough. The work left an island where they built a slip, which was soon to be managed by J E Harland.

Sometimes described as 'Belfast by the Sea', Bangor is a busy industrial town and seaside resort situated on Belfast Lough, at the north end of the Ards peninsula. It was the site of a great 6th-century abbey, a sacred site of the Celtic Catholic Church, which was founded by St Comgall. During the 6th century many of St Comgall's followers set out on missionary journeys in their coracles from a rocky reef near Bangor's steamer pier. A number of western Europe's monasteries were founded by these monks from Bangor. The abbey was sacked by the Danes and, although re-founded later, was eventually dissolved by Henry VIII. The present town was founded by Sir James Hamilton for Scottish settlers in the early 17th century.

BANGOR, THE ESPLANADE 1897 40241

CARRICKFERGUS, LOOKING NORTH EAST 1897 40282

The singer and songwriter Van Morrison was born in Belfast in 1945. His music has been influenced by his cultural heritage, for apart from hits such as 'Brown-Eyed Girl' and 'Moondance', strongly influenced by American musical styles, other work shows the influence of Celtic tradition and jazz, such as 'Astral Weeks' and 'Veedon Fleece'. This influence is sometimes referred to as 'Celtic Soul'. Morrison was inducted into the Rock and Roll Hall of Fame, and was ranked 25 in the American music channel Vh1's list of the 100 Greatest Artists of Rock and Roll.

100 years after the Normans defeated the English at the battle of Hastings in 1066 they had ambitions to conquer Ireland. Their military system required castles to proclaim dominion, and the huge slab of rock jutting into what is now known as Belfast Lough and named Krag Fergus gave an ideal site. The Normans established a town around Carrickfergus Castle and the church, dedicated to St Nicholas. The stones were to witness turmoil and violence over many centuries. Photograph 40276, below, was taken from the old pier where William III landed in Ireland on his way to do battle at the Boyne.

The town of Carrickfergus became busy and prosperous, with markets twice a week and five linen mills needing workers. The harbour would have exported rock salt, taken from four deep mines, to be processed across the water; the linen would have gone by rail to the specialised warehouses in Belfast. The main line belonged to the Belfast and Northern Counties Railway, but there was a locally-owned Carrickfergus Harbour Junction Railway.

CARRICKFERGUS CASTLE 1897 40276

The quay at Carrickfergus seen in this photograph was built in 1830 for the men who lived in the overlooking Scotch Corner. When this photograph was taken the fishing industry was no

CARRICKFERGUS, FISHERMAN'S QUAY 1897 40281

longer important, but according to a local historian of the time it had once provided work for something like 300 people, counting those employed on secondary parts like net-making.

LISBURN, MARKET SQUARE 1896 L138001

Now a suburb of Belfast, the town of Lisburn in the Lagan valley was originally colonised by English and Welsh settlers. Ulster's Irish Linen industry began at Lisburn, when the French Huguenot refugee Louis Crommelin arrived with the latest expertise in making linen. Lisburn's church was granted cathedral status in 1662, and its structure is an example of Plantation Gothic. The tower seen in photograph L138001, above, with its clock and cupola, marks a market house and assembly rooms. The cast iron fountain on the right of the photograph was commissioned by Sir Richard Wallace (1818-90), who was a native of Lisburn. It was one of 50 or so which Sir Richard commissioned; most of them were erected in Paris, where he lived, to celebrate the end of the siege of the city by the Prussians in 1871.

Recorded on the tomb of Katherine Leary in Belfast:

Beneath this stone lies Katherine my wife,
In death my comfort, and my plague through life,
Oh, liberty! But soft, I must not boast,
She'll haunt me else, by jingo, with her ghost!

It was a ford which fixed the site of Belfast, but not long after the town was begun a bridge crossed the river. The approach to it, Ann Street, was the second most important thoroughfare, and beyond the bridge it took the name Bridge End. Visible in the background of photograph 40188, below, is a 120ft-high glass kiln that was already 100 years old at this time, and the tall chimneys show that Ballymacarret had other industries.

ANN STREET 1897 40188

THE ULSTER INSTITUTE FOR THE DEAF, DUMB AND BLIND 1897 40202

The 225ft frontage of the Ulster Institute for the Deaf, Dumb and Blind, seen in photograph 40202, above, along with the two wings extending to the rear, shows what had to, and could, be achieved by charity. The Institute catered for those needing help from all over the province.

In 1859 Edward James Harland went into business with Gustav Wolff, and one of the world's largest shipyards was born, Harland & Wolff of Belfast. This yard was to build some of the most famous ships in the world, such as the 'Oceanic' and the 'Olympic'. However the most famous ship of all to come out of the Harland & Wolff yard was the ill-fated 'Titanic', which struck an iceberg and sank on her maiden voyage in 1912. Many Belfast people are descended from the workforce who built the 'Titanic', and there is a memorial to the doomed liner in the city centre.

In 1832 the Seamen's Friendly Society was set up, and by 1836 it had a small building of its own in Pilot Street. In 1848 it became part of the Presbyterian Church in Ireland, and a few years later it was decided that there should be a new congregation. At the same time a wealthy shipper died, and his widow asked for a church to be built in his memory. The Sinclair Seamen's Presbyterian Church is the work of the leading Belfast architect John Lanyon. The minister was always to devote part of his time to seamen, and 50 seats were reserved for sailors. A few years later, the church came under the care of a man who began to furnish the interior with nautical emblems. The bowsprit pulpit is still there, complete with bow and starboard lights.

The Palm House in the Botanic Gardens was designed by Sir Charles Lanyon, who became Mayor of Belfast in 1862 and Member of Parliament in 1866. It is one of the earliest curvilinear glass houses to have been built, and is the oldest still standing today. The foundation stone was laid in 1839, nine years before the Great Palm House at Kew in England; both Palm Houses were built by Richard Turner of Dublin. The dome was designed in 1862.

THE BOTANIC GARDENS, THE CONSERVATORY 1936 87687

A VIEW OF CAVE HILL 1897 40217

Cave Hill was traditionally the scene of festivities on Easter Monday. The poet William Reed described the scene in 1818:

Now group on group is seen to follow far
Like a rabble army in array -
On foot, on horse, coach, jingle cart and car;
Towards the Hill of Caves they wend their way...
Here you might mark life's anxious, ardent strugglers
Of every hue - whate'er their cast or calling -
Musicians, pedlars, show-men, dupes and jugglers -
No Babel tower had echoed to such bawling!
Carousing, begging, singing, dancing, brawling,
The fiddle's flourish, and the bagpipe's grunting....

Situated about five miles to the east of Belfast and built in neo-classical style, Stormont (photograph 87696, below) was the home of the Northern Irish Parliament until 1972, when it was suspended. The parliament was subsequently abolished under the Constitution of Northern Ireland Act, 1973. Stormont is now the home of the Northern Ireland Assembly created under the Belfast Agreement of 1998.

STORMONT 1936 87696

SPORTING BELFAST

Although the Ireland international rugby team is an All-Ireland team, it is over 50 years since an international fixture was played in Belfast. The last game took place in the 1953-54 season, a defeat to Scotland at the Ravenhill ground. However, there are now plans for an international quality stadium at Maysfield, which could bring the Irish team back to the city.

Linfield FC have an extraordinary history of success, and in the 2005-06 season were the holders of the All-Ireland Setanta Cup, the League Cup and the County Antrim Shield. Their League Championship win in 2003-04 was their 200th trophy. They had two other spectacularly successful seasons: in 1921-22 they won all seven competitions that they entered, and in 1961-62 they won seven trophies, but failed to make it 8 out of 8 when they lost to Glentoran in the International Cup.

Queens University, Belfast, has produced three Olympic medal winners. Billy McConnel won bronze at Los Angeles in 1984 in hockey; Jimmy Kirkwood won gold at Seoul in 1988 in hockey; and Thelma Hopkins won silver at Melbourne in 1956 in the long jump.

The boxer Wayne McCullough, born in Belfast in 1970, won the WBC world title in the Bantamweight category in 1995, beating the champion Yasuei Yakushiji in Nagoya, Japan. As an amateur McCullough won a gold medal at the 1990 Commonwealth Games in Auckland, representing Northern Ireland, and a silver medal for Ireland at the 1992 Barcelona Olympics. He also won a bronze medal at the World Cup before moving from Northern Ireland to Las Vegas to begin a professional career.

Belfast has produced not one but two of the most famous footballers in sporting history, Danny Blanchflower and George Best.

Blanchflower (born in Belfast in 1926) captained Tottenham Hotspur during their double-winning season of 1961. He is remembered as one of the great tacticians in the history of the game, renowned for his passing, and as an outstanding right-half. When he captained Spurs to victory over Atletico Madrid in the final of the 1963 European Cup Winners' Cup, they became the first British side to win a European trophy. Between 1949 and 1963, he earned 56 caps for Northern Ireland, often playing alongside his brother Jackie, and in 1958 captained his country when they reached the quarter-finals of the World Cup. He retired as a player in 1964, but returned to the game briefly as manager of Northern Ireland in 1978, and then Chelsea in 1978-79. He summed up his approach to the game as: 'Football is about glory; it is about doing things in style and with a flourish, about going out and beating the lot, not waiting for them to die of boredom.'

George Best, born in Belfast in 1946, is widely acknowledged to have been one of the greatest football players of all time. His days of glory were with Manchester United FC between 1963 and 1974, and although he played for the Northern Ireland team, their failure to reach the final rounds of the World Cup denied him the ultimate global stage he deserved. He helped Manchester United to win the Football League Championship in 1965 and 1967, and the European Cup in 1968, and was named European Footballer of the Year and Football Writers' Association Player of the Year in 1968. His combination of pace, sure-footedness, goal-scoring skills and ability to run through defences earned him the respect of players of all nations. The great Brazilian player Pelé called him 'the greatest footballer in the world'. After retiring from top-level football, Best fought a long battle against alcoholism, eventually dying in 2005, aged 59. He was buried in East Belfast after a moving funeral; thousands of people lined the streets on a rainy day to say goodbye to one of the city's best-known sons.

QUIZ QUESTIONS

Answers on page 49.

1. How did Belfast benefit from the American Civil War?

2. Where in Belfast can couples tie a nautical knot when they marry?

3. Where and what is Napoleon's Nose?

4. Who was said to have 'ice in his veins, warmth in his heart, and timing and balance in his feet'?

5. What was unusual about the medal presentation ceremony when Wayne McCullough won a gold medal for Northern Ireland in the Featherweight Boxing event at the 1990 Commonwealth Games?

6. Whose catchphrase is 'It's a cracker!'?

7. What is the link between Belfast, a lion and a wardrobe?

8. What is the third most commonly spoken language in Northern Ireland, after English and Irish?

9. Which Belfast pub was once a lock-up for unwilling tourists to Australia?

10. Where in Belfast could you go to have your spots and warts removed?

VICTORIA STREET 1897 40179

RECIPE

POTATO FARLS

This potato cake or bread is an essential part of an Ulster Fry breakfast. The mashed potatoes should be freshly cooked and mashed, never prepared in advance.

Ingredients

2lb/1kg cooked and mashed potatoes
4oz/125g plain flour
2 tablespoons melted butter
Salt to taste
Fat or oil for frying

Mix the melted butter into the potatoes with the salt. Work in the flour, and knead the mixture lightly. Divide the mixture into two portions, and roll each out on a floured board to form a round about 12 inches (30cm) across. Cut into quarters (these are the 'farls'), and fry for a few minutes on each side, in a small amount of fat or oil - bacon fat is the best for flavour and authenticity.

RECIPE

CHAMP

Champ is an Irish mashed potato dish that is most usually served heaped on a plate with 1-2 tablespoons of butter melting in the middle; the mashed potatoes are eaten from the outside to the inside, dipping each forkful into the butter.

Ingredients

8 medium potatoes, peeled and cut into chunks
¼ pint/125ml milk
Salt and pepper
1 bunch spring onions (scallions), sliced
1 knob of butter per person, to serve

Cook the potatoes in a pot of boiling water until very tender (about 15 minutes).

While the potatoes are cooking, in a small saucepan bring the milk to a simmer over medium heat, stirring often; add the chopped spring onions (scallions) to the milk, remove from heat; cover with lid and let them steep (off the heat) while the potatoes are cooking.

When cooked, drain the potatoes thoroughly, then return to the same pot and mash with a potato masher (do not beat, leave the potatoes with some small chunks). Add in the milk and onion mixture; mix with a wooden spoon to combine. Season with salt and pepper to taste. Spoon the mashed potatoes onto each plate in a pile, and make an indentation.

Put 1-2 tablespoons butter in the indentation, and serve immediately whilst still hot.

BANGOR, THE ESPLANADE 1897 40253

QUIZ ANSWERS

1. Belfast's linen industry prospered during the period of the American Civil War, because the Lancashire cotton industry was short of its raw material during the Union blockade of the cotton fields of the South, and had to scale down production.

2. Sinclair Seamen's Presbyterian Church in Corporation Street is full of nautical items, including a linoleum anchor at the altar for the bride and groom to stand on during the wedding service, to symbolise that they are 'safely anchored for life'.

3. Belfast is overlooked by Cave Hill, which has the silhouette of a human face and has been nicknamed 'Napoleon's Nose'.

4. The Belfast-born footballer George Best, as described by another Belfast footballing hero, Danny Blanchflower.

5. As McCullough was presented with his medal, a technical problem with the public address system made it impossible to play the recording of the Northern Ireland anthem. The New Zealand official in charge of the sound promptly jumped into the ring, took the microphone and sang the anthem unaccompanied.

6. The Belfast-born comedian Frank Carson.

7. The author Clive Staples Lewis, commonly referred to as C S Lewis, who was born in Belfast in 1898. He is best known for his series of children's books about the magical kingdom of Narnia, one of which, 'The Lion, The Witch and the Wardrobe', was recently turned into a successful film.

8. Cantonese, mostly due to the considerable Chinese community of Belfast, which has more Chinese restaurants per capita than any other European city.

9. The Rotterdam Bar in Belfast's docklands, which was once a prison for convicts awaiting transportation to Australia.

10. St Matthew's Church on the Woodvale Road in Belfast, where a 'bullaun' (hollowed out) stone near the door is said to have the power to cure warts, spots and acne.

THE ALBERT MEMORIAL CLOCK AND TOWER 1897 40182

BELFAST CASTLE AND LOUGH 1897 40214

FRANCIS FRITH

PIONEER VICTORIAN PHOTOGRAPHER

Francis Frith, founder of the world-famous photographic archive, was a complex and multi-talented man. A devout Quaker and a highly successful Victorian businessman, he was philosophical by nature and pioneering in outlook. By 1855 he had already established a wholesale grocery business in Liverpool, and sold it for the astonishing sum of £200,000, which is the equivalent today of over £15,000,000. Now in his thirties, and captivated by the new science of photography, Frith set out on a series of pioneering journeys up the Nile and to the Near East.

INTRIGUE AND EXPLORATION

He was the first photographer to venture beyond the sixth cataract of the Nile. Africa was still the mysterious 'Dark Continent', and Stanley and Livingstone's historic meeting was a decade into the future. The conditions for picture taking confound belief. He laboured for hours in his wicker dark-room in the sweltering heat of the desert, while the volatile chemicals fizzed dangerously in their trays. Back in London he exhibited his photographs and was 'rapturously cheered' by members of the Royal Society. His reputation as a photographer was made overnight.

VENTURE OF A LIFE-TIME

By the 1870s the railways had threaded their way across the country, and Bank Holidays and half-day Saturdays had been made obligatory by Act of Parliament. All of a sudden the working man and his family were able to enjoy days out, take holidays, and see a little more of the world.

With typical business acumen, Francis Frith foresaw that these new tourists would enjoy having souvenirs to commemorate their days out. For the next thirty years he travelled the country by train and by pony and trap, producing fine photographs of seaside resorts and beauty spots that were keenly bought by millions of Victorians. These prints were painstakingly pasted into family albums and pored over during the dark nights of winter, rekindling precious memories of summer excursions. Frith's studio was soon supplying retail shops all over the country, and by 1890 F Frith & Co had become the greatest specialist photographic publishing company in the world, with over 2,000 sales outlets, and pioneered the picture postcard.

FRANCIS FRITH'S LEGACY

Francis Frith had died in 1898 at his villa in Cannes, his great project still growing. By 1970 the archive he created contained over a third of a million pictures showing 7,000 British towns and villages.

Frith's legacy to us today is of immense significance and value, for the magnificent archive of evocative photographs he created provides a unique record of change in the cities, towns and villages throughout Britain over a century and more. Frith and his fellow studio photographers revisited locations many times down the years to update their views, compiling for us an enthralling and colourful pageant of British life and character.

We are fortunate that Frith was dedicated to recording the minutiae of everyday life. For it is this sheer wealth of visual data, the painstaking chronicle of changes in dress, transport, street layouts, buildings, housing and landscape that captivates us so much today, offering us a powerful link with the past and with the lives of our ancestors.

Computers have now made it possible for Frith's many thousands of images to be accessed almost instantly. The archive offers every one of us an opportunity to examine the places where we and our families have lived and worked down the years. Its images, depicting our shared past, are now bringing pleasure and enlightenment to millions around the world a century and more after his death.

For further information visit: www.francisfrith.com

INTERIOR DECORATION

Frith's photographs can be seen framed and as giant wall murals in thousands of pubs, restaurants, hotels, banks, retail stores and other public buildings throughout Britain. These provide interesting and attractive décor, generating strong local interest and acting as a powerful reminder of gentler days in our increasingly busy and frenetic world.

FRITH PRODUCTS

All Frith photographs are available as prints and posters in a variety of different sizes and styles. In the UK we also offer a range of other gift and stationery products illustrated with Frith photographs, although many of these are not available for delivery outside the UK – see our web site for more information on the products available for delivery in your country.

THE INTERNET

Over 100,000 photographs of Britain can be viewed and purchased on the Frith web site. The web site also includes memories and reminiscences contributed by our customers, who have personal knowledge of localities and of the people and properties depicted in Frith photographs. If you wish to learn more about a specific town or village you may find these reminiscences fascinating to browse. Why not add your own comments if you think they would be of interest to others? See **www.francisfrith.com**

PLEASE HELP US BRING FRITH'S PHOTOGRAPHS TO LIFE

Our authors do their best to recount the history of the places they write about. They give insights into how particular towns and villages developed, they describe the architecture of streets and buildings, and they discuss the lives of famous people who lived there. But however knowledgeable our authors are, the story they tell is necessarily incomplete.

Frith's photographs are so much more than plain historical documents. They are living proofs of the flow of human life down the generations. They show real people at real moments in history; and each of those people is the son or daughter of someone, the brother or sister, aunt or uncle, grandfather or grandmother of someone else. All of them lived, worked and played in the streets depicted in Frith's photographs.

We would be grateful if you would give us your insights into the places shown in our photographs: the streets and buildings, the shops, businesses and industries. Post your memories of life in those streets on the Frith website: what it was like growing up there, who ran the local shop and what shopping was like years ago; if your workplace is shown tell us about your working day and what the building is used for now. Read other visitors' memories and reconnect with your shared local history and heritage. With your help more and more Frith photographs can be brought to life, and vital memories preserved for posterity, and for the benefit of historians in the future.

Wherever possible, we will try to include some of your comments in future editions of our books. Moreover, if you spot errors in dates, titles or other facts, please let us know, because our archive records are not always completely accurate—they rely on 140 years of human endeavour and hand-compiled records. You can email us using the contact form on the website.

Thank you!

For further information, trade, or author enquiries please contact us at the address below:

The Francis Frith Collection, Oakley Business Park, Wylye Road, Dinton, Wiltshire SP3 5EU.

Tel: +44 (0)1722 716 376 Fax: +44 (0)1722 716 881

e-mail: sales@francisfrith.co.uk **www.francisfrith.com**